There is a Higher Power Within

28 Meditation Prompts to Find Peace &
Happiness Within

I0190566

By

Ana Barreto, MBA

Books by Ana Barreto

Women, Rice and Beans: Nine Wisdoms I Learned from My Mother When I Really Paid Attention

Self-trust: A Healing Practice for Women Who Do Too Much

1st Edition, March 2020
ISBN-13: 978-0-9979006-7-5
ISBN-10: 0-9979006-7-5
Blue Hudson Group, Rhinebeck, NY

Dedication

To my mother Aracy, who has shown me how to partner with the Holy Spirit

during times of turbulence.

To my teachers who, through their teachings, books, classes, and coaching, have guided me

to find all I needed within.

On Meditation

When I meditate, I become open and available to discover the path life is taking me on: The path that I created. I surrender and let go of the expectations I have written on stones. My load becomes lighter, and I embrace the journey, knowing that something better is waiting for me.

The signs are everywhere, and this time, I'm able to understand. Enthusiasm arrives at my doorstep, and I can't wait until the next morning when once again, I meet myself, my Creator, and Humanity in the moments of stillness.

Introduction

This is a pause. A moment when you snooze your discontent just like you do with your alarm clock in the morning as you attempt to delay the start of your day. But instead of giving yourself a few more minutes to sleep, I'm inviting you to snooze your clock for meditation.

Doing so will change your life. It's like Science and Religion had a child called Meditation. The physical and spiritual benefits of time spent in stillness or contemplation are endless. From reduced stress to lowered blood pressure, to improved emotional intelligence to spiritual healing, meditation is the cure the world has been looking for.

This book is the result of a collaboration with the Holy Spirit. Our intention is to help you find peace and happiness in your life with a regular practice of eight minutes or more over a period of time to connect with your power within.

You see, there's a Higher Power within you, which is within everyone. You only need to know that It exists. You can connect with It and put It to good use. Meditation will help you do that, while helping you improve the quality of your life and dissolving your discontent.

If you're a beginner who has never practiced meditation before, this is a great place to start. It may seem to you that you aren't doing much, but that's when you know you're doing right. In truth, no one can practice meditation the wrong way. You can begin with the eight minutes and extend it as you progress.

If you're an irregular practitioner, this meditation format will help you practice more regularly. With time, you will know, own, and honor your own personal practice. If you're practicing meditation for 15 to 20 minutes already, feel free to extend it.

If you're an experienced practitioner, the meditation prompts here will guide you into a higher contemplation state. That's when profound changes happen quickly.

Know that with 30 minutes or more of stillness, you can access high states of bliss, direct guidance, and enormous levels of compassion. These states lead to faster miracles.

These daily practices that last a minimum of eight minutes will change the trajectory of your day, your week, your year, and ultimately, your life.

You may wonder how a pause in your day could change the conditions of your life so dramatically, but it's simple. Everything starts small, and small things can create a tsunami. Of course, no one wants a tsunami to take over their life, but creating these small mindful stops at the beginning and end of your day will positively transform your life experience as if a tsunami went by.

Based on my experience, the first level of transformation is subtle. You're simply centered, calm, and relaxed. In these states of being, you'll have access to higher creativity and insights. In the next level, the things that used to push your "overreact" buttons won't bother you as much. Over time, your thinking will become clearer. Your emotions will be present, but you won't burn others with unfitting displays that harm more than build. It will seem as though you're stepping outside of yourself, seeing life's events from a different perspective and receiving direct guidance on how to be and take action.

The practice is simple. If you're a beginner, you meditate for six to eight minutes in the morning when you first wake up and for two minutes at night before bed. Then, lengthen your practice as time goes on or how you see fit.

I suggest that you set your alarm clock for eight to fifteen minutes before you normally get up. When the alarm goes off, your practice begins.

The Morning:

1. Snooze your alarm.

2. Sit down, and take three deep and long breaths.

3. Read one of the Meditation Prompts. (One through Twenty-Eight).

4. Contemplate the thought or image the meditation prompt gives. Keep breathing until the alarm goes off.

Don't worry if your mind wanders because it probably will. When you notice it wandering, say to yourself: ***"Be still. I am with Spirit."*** Then, go back to contemplating the prompt, and keep breathing.

The Evening:

1. While you're in bed, take three deep and long breaths.
2. Read the Moment of Gratitude Prompt.
3. Go to sleep.

As you begin this practice, many of the prompts will stay with you during the day. You may feel a pull to go back to the previous meditation prompt the next day or be with the thought all day for a few days. You may open the book randomly and select any of the twenty-eight meditation prompts. There are no rules. Trust your intuition. In fact, as you begin a regular meditation practice, you'll be guided to a fast path to your intentions because you're eliminating the distractions every morning when you meet with yourself.

Wake up and Meditate

When you meditate in the morning upon first waking up before your mind move into a beta frequency (the state of constant chatting and habitual survival mode), you elevate your energy to high level feelings of well-being. Your intuition improves, and you feel centered and ready to walk into your day without hurry. Also, you are less influenced by things that used to upset you.

After a while, you will notice that you're operating from such a level of happiness, peace, and enthusiasm that some people, things, and events that don't match your higher state of being won't affect your experience.

Meditation also increases the thickness of your prefrontal cortex, the area of your brain associated with attention and self-awareness. You can begin to watch yourself improve your behavior, acting on your intentions. Many people experience being nudged to take an action or make a decision they were avoiding. Meditation also makes your brain more coherent.

Morning Meditation helps you create your day. Everyone creates their life unconsciously, but with meditation, you become a deliberate creator. Many people wake up in the morning dreading the workday, and as they go about their day, they witness what they created when they first woke up—dread. They blame others, of course, but they unintentionally created it themselves.

When you begin your morning meditation with a prompt, you are led to the thought of the day which is intended to build on peace, happiness, love, spirituality, compassion, and good deeds. Do you know a better way to start and create your day?

Evening Meditation

People often end the day with a television show that only increases the anxiety they experienced during the day. How about ending the day on a high note, such as a state of gratitude? When we feel grateful, it's impossible for us to feel angry or mad. Gratitude softens our attitude and allows us to be open to receive.

The last thought of the day tends to influence our dreams. If you could select your dreams, would you rather receive troubles or solutions?

There's a good chance you've been told about meditation before, read articles, or even watched an interview about meditation in the past. You may still believe that you don't know how to meditate, can't quiet your mind, or don't have the time. I'm here to tell you that you can do it. It's time to release the obstacles you created to finding peace and happiness in your life. It's time to meet with yourself and access your power.

So you've been nudged again to meditate. Begin slowly with no expectations. This is not a pass or fail test. Your life will change. Every meditator's life has. It's now your turn.

To start, read the next few pages the night before you begin with Meditation Prompt One. Then, enjoy the journey.

The Breath

Begin by taking three breaths. Your body and mind remember their wisdom. Each breath is an act of kindness to the self and to Humanity.

The breath has power and is often underestimated. Even the shallowest of breaths are powerful enough to...

Guide you to make mindful decisions;

Lead you to connect with your passion;

Bring you to release stress from your body;

Convince you to surrender to peace;

Disarm you to align with a Higher Power;

Carry you to promote life;

Sway you to exchange energy with the trees.

If you encounter the "darkest hours," turn on the light. It's only one deep breath away.

"Be Still. 1 Am with Spirit."

Our mind wanders. It's the nature of the mind. With stillness, the mind sees a trap, as it cannot express itself. Say with authority and kindness: BE STILL.

We need the quietness so wisdom can surface through the Higher Power.

Don't fight with the mind. You will not win. It's best to persuade it with repetition:

BE STILL. I AM WITH SPIRIT.

GOD

There is a Higher Power in all life. People may call it God, Universe, Jehovah, Param Brahma, Elohim, Allah, Mother, Father, Gaia, and other names.

But meditation is not a religion. It's one of the many ways you can connect with the power of the Spirit.

In the end, we are all ONE, united by the Spirit, having different experiences and the innate intention of improving the conditions of all Humanity.

ONE

Every day is a new beginning. Today is an opportunity to begin a relationship with Me, which is a relationship with you and everything in the Universe. Tap into your heart, and that's my hand. It's going to be an amazing journey.

Moment of Gratitude

Today, I am grateful for being alive.

TWO

God sits on the edge of your bed in awe of His creation.
Do you agree with Him?

You are perfect.

A Moment of Gratitude

Today, I am grateful for my body, mind and wisdom.

THREE

It isn't your hair, your eyes, or the color of your skin that makes you sacred.

It's your pure existence. Your breath is His divine essence.

A Moment of Gratitude

Today, I am grateful for breathing.

FOUR

My Hands are your hands. My Fingers are your fingers.
Always choose to build instead of destroy, or WE will
need to build it again.

A Moment of Gratitude

Today, I am grateful for OUR hands.

FIVE

Look up. What do you see? The ceiling, the sky, or all the imperfections? Be mindful of what you choose to see, as those choices become OUR world.

A Moment of Gratitude

Today, I am grateful for my eyes and the ability to
witness the creation of Our world.

SIX

Feel your feet on the floor. Is it cold, warm, rough, smooth, clean, or dirty? It is supporting your weight with the best conditions WE have created thus far.

Your steps are OUR steps. Although it may not seem like it,

WE are always moving forward.

A Moment of Gratitude

Today, I am grateful for the detours I created in OUR life.

I was being asked to slow down.

SEVEN

God caresses your head every morning before you wake up to remind you that you can surrender and let go of worries. You are exactly where you need to be today, and WE are working toward accepting it.

A Moment of Gratitude

Today, I am grateful for the relief I'm able to receive,
which is always available to me.

The Mind

Once your mind is stretched by a new experience, your mind can never go back to the old dimensions of existence. The Universe is always preparing you for what you asked. If you asked for peace, be prepared to let go of what brings you chaos. If you asked for happiness, be prepared to let go of what makes you sad. The Universe may be freeing you from the people closest to you and the environment you grew accustomed to.

EIGHT

My hair is growing uncontrolled by me. My fingernails, too. My heart beats without my command. There is intelligence inside of me that creates a world just for me.

A Moment of Gratitude

Today, I am grateful to know that life still happens
without my input.

NINE

My eyes may not be perfect, but my vision has a choice. I can always choose to see a new reality with attention to my intention.

A Moment of Gratitude

Today, I create my world with one intention at a time.

TEN

The energy of my words can build or destroy my
Universe. When I think, the transformation begins.
When I speak, I set my fate in gear.

A Moment of Gratitude

Today, I choose to build myself a better world with my words.

ELEVEN

The stillness of every morning is an invitation to inhabit the peace within. Before chasing problems to solve when the sun rises, I let the problems run wild into the fire. I don't have to solve them all.

A Moment of Gratitude

Today, I am grateful for the immense peace available to me.

TWELVE

Worries are like a woodpecker pecking on a house made of wood. They will keep coming back unless I address the source of the problem. Worries damage our inner peace, even though most of them never come to pass. It's time to release worries and trust OUR inner wisdom.

A Moment of Gratitude

Today, I choose to trust myself and release the source of my worries.

THIRTEEN

Fear has an opinion about everything. My pessimistic views of the world call for more acts of self-love and kindness. I can release my fears and trust that the Universe is working on my behalf.

A Moment of Gratitude

Today, I hear with gratitude the points my fear wants me to acknowledge. Then, I choose to honor that fear is a call for self-love.

FOURTEEN

Light is our essence. This means that the darkness we
attract helps us appreciate our core state of being.

A Moment of Gratitude

Today, I commit to remembering my light during my
darkest moments and knowing that I am a source of
light.

Intention

Everything we believe we need is already available to us by the power of our intentions. In order to receive, we must let go of the thoughts "I don't have it" or "It's too hard" and be absolutely clear about what we want.

Know that the Universe does not judge your intentions; people do.

Be mindful of the sudden thoughts you have about your intentions. These only delay the process. In meditation, you can be truthful about your expectations. Expect your intentions, and the world will unfold for you with a reality better than you expected.

FIFTEEN

The fog is not a barrier. It's a pause. We can't see clearly, so it's time to surrender and slow down.

A Moment of Gratitude

Today, I am grateful for the things I can't yet understand.

SIXTEEN

The biggest act of kindness we can do for Humanity is to live on purpose. Our purpose is never for us, but to serve others without leaving ourselves behind. This is what brings meaning to our lives.

A Moment of Gratitude

Today, I am grateful and open to guidance as to how to serve deeper, fuller, and effortlessly, without depletion.

SEVENTEEN

"I am open to receive" is the most important mantra.

I surrender to the abundant life I am creating.

A Moment of Gratitude

Today, I am grateful for the prosperity I see in my life.

EIGHTEEN

Some creatures are born with wings they don't know
how to use until they are pushed out of the nest. You
were born with wings you don't know how to use until
you are out of your comfort zone.

A Moment of Gratitude

Today, I am open to stepping outside my comfort zone.

NINETEEN

The Spirit woke me up and said: *We only thrive with compassion.*

I understood and slept in that morning.

A Moment of Gratitude

Today, I am grateful for my ability to practice self-compassion.

TWENTY

All work produced from a state of depletion can never be inspirational. When we choose to serve, it must come from, and continue to expand with, joy.

A Moment of Gratitude

Today, I give myself time to restore.

TWENTY-ONE

Strength doesn't come from what you can do. It comes from overcoming what you once thought you couldn't overcome. Remember to call on your Higher Power.

A Moment of Gratitude

Today, I am grateful for the powers I didn't know existed in me.

Peace

What is Peace?

The Spirit said that Peace is the space between now and the next moment. It's a brief moment of surrender that can last longer than anyone ever lived.

Peace is often forgotten until something falls apart. Then, we call and expect her to drop everything and answer our needs at a moment's notice.

We cry for her from the top of our lungs on every mountaintop and from the bottom of the oceans like a jealous lover. We can't hear her and wonder "where is Peace?"

The problem is that Peace is never away from us. We look "out there," but she lives within. Peace has only one message: Be okay with the best and worst-case scenarios, and you will have me.

Peace is a state of being.

TWENTY-TWO

Be aware of the actions you take because of fear.

Don't get up in the morning because you're afraid of the consequences of being late. Get up because you want to be happy, and have a relaxed morning that lingers in the shower. Your journey will then carry a different flavor.

A Moment of Gratitude

Today, I am grateful for the happy thoughts I set in the morning.

TWENTY-THREE

Don't be afraid to start over. You are never starting from scratch. You are starting with new wisdom. See the doors that have closed as a blessing.

If you look for them, you will find the blessings within.

A Moment of Gratitude

Today, I am grateful for all the blessed hands I have received.

TWENTY-FOUR

If you erase all the mistakes of your past, you will also erase all the wisdom of your present. Remember the lessons and not the disappointments. That's how we grow.

A Moment of Gratitude

Today, with gratitude, I release the need to remember my hurts.

If I can't, I will study the lessons.

TWENTY-FIVE

When we need to take a big step, there may be a voice inside that says: "You are not quite ready." But there will be another that will reply: "Be brave."

The voice that you listen to can bring you peace or war. The Universe responds to bravery. WE are never deserted.

A Moment of Gratitude

Today. I am grateful for partnering with my bravery in every action

that I expect to be difficult.

TWENTY-SIX

You don't need to forgive anyone if you understand that ALL is love, and WE are one. Remember that for every person you forgive, you heal your own wounds.

A Moment of Gratitude

Today, I gratefully accept that all hurts are self-inflicted.
I have a choice of how I respond to the world.

TWENTY-SEVEN

Your intuition is a gift. It's a power that will always lead to safety. Learn to discern this voice from the voice of your insecurities. Peace is always on the agenda when you honor your gifts.

A Moment of Gratitude

Today, I gratefully call my intuition forward and
become more intimate in our relationship.

TWENTY-EIGHT

Your voice is MY voice. Your thoughts are MY thoughts. To sync OUR state of peace and happiness, WE just need to be still and know that WE are ONE. I am your Spirit-self. I'm here to guide you and remind you of your divinity.

Be still and listen to your breath. God breathes through you. Every cell of your body is the essence of God.

Wake up OUR power by inviting peace and happiness into your world.

A Moment of Gratitude

Today, I am grateful for feeling the essence of God in my life.

Compassion

Compassion is more than a word. It's a power. Often in meditation, we stumble upon compassion, which means "to suffer together." It seems like God played a trick on Humanity because compassion can only be expressed once we have experienced pain.

We grow Compassion when we connect with Humanity. Compassion allows us to be in the highest state of the human condition. Compassion is a practical power. When we don't understand this power, we are simply giving it away.

I invite you to feel self-compassion, as this helps everyone. Intend to have more peace and happiness in your life. The next time you encounter Compassion on your meditation road, allow it to enter your inner door. Once you feel it, you will know that you are worthy of peace and happiness, not just in drops at times, but eternally.

Resources

Join our Body, Mind & Wisdom Community on Facebook for insights, inspiration, and support. We host private classes and share unique content daily.
Facebook Group: BMWisdom

For Guided Meditations:

Visit www.ana-barreto.com/meditations

How to connect online:

Visit www.ana-barreto.com

Like my page on Facebook: @ana1barreto

Follow me on Instagram: @ana1barreto

Follow me on twitter: @ana1barreto

Follow me on Pinterest: @ana1barreto

Send your comments, questions, and concerns to ana@ana-barreto.com

Share the Word!

About the Author

Ana Barreto is a Brazilian-American teacher, author, and coach living in upstate New York. She grew up in Rio de Janeiro, Brazil. At eighteen years of age, she left her parents' traditional patriarchal home, breaking the established female roles in her own house. Two years later, she moved to New York and began her college education.

While attending Marymount College, at that time a women's only institution, Ana began to learn about women's rights and empowerment. Her passion for women's development and growth led her to study psychology, women's history, women in business, women and leadership, meditation, spirituality, and Eastern philosophies. She holds Bachelor's and Master's degrees in Business Administration.

Ana published her first book *Women, Rice and Beans – Nine Wisdoms I Learned from My Mother When I Really*

Paid Attention in 2016. She hopes to inspire women who are overwhelmed in their own lives to find daily wisdom and break old patterns of thinking, believing, and being that don't honor their Spirit.

In her second book *Self-Trust – A Healing Practice for Women Who Work Too Much* published in 2018, Ana shares sixteen healing practices to help women trust themselves and change old mindset patterns that don't serve Humanity.

Ana's purpose is to help people improve the quality of their lives. Her mission is to inspire, guide, and coach women through her books, classes, meditations, and inspirational material to find their inner compass and live a great life.

When Ana isn't working or writing books, she likes cooking, traveling, hiking, biking, kayaking, and spending time with her partner, Jim; daughters Erica and Isabel; step daughters Cindy, Janet, and Christine; and friends.